RYUHO
OKAWA

THE MOMENT *of* TRUTH

BECOME A LIVING ANGEL TODAY

IRH PRESS

The material in this book is selected from various talks given by
Ryuho Okawa to a live audience

RO Books is a registered trademark of IRH Press Co., Ltd.

IRH PRESS

New York ~ Tokyo

Distributed by National Book Network Inc.   www.nbnbooks.com

Library of Congress Catalog Card Number: 2011924426

ISBN 13: 978-0-9826985-7-0
ISBN 10: 0-9826985-7-7

Printed in USA

Cover Design: LeVan Fisher Design
Book Design: Bookcraft Ltd
Cover Image: Roc Canals Photography/Getty Images

CONTENTS

CHAPTER SIX:
Q&A WITH MASTER OKAWA

PREFACE

This book is a record of my determination to spread my teachings, even at the cost of my life. In November 2010, with a firm resolve, I traveled halfway around the world to Brazil and delivered a series of five talks in one week. This was an endeavor that I wanted to accomplish at all costs. Just before I left for Brazil, I held a talk for my disciples to leave with them my last words, in case anything should happen to me. I wanted to be sure that I had told them everything I could before I left.

On my way, the flight had a four-hour layover in the Dallas airport for refueling. My heart was already so impassioned with a sense of mission that I told my secretaries that I wanted to give a talk immediately, right in the airport. When my troubled staff told me I had no followers living in Dallas, I exclaimed, "That's fine; then go find me some scorpions for an audience!"

This book is a compilation of lectures delivered to a Brazilian audience. However, I gave these talks with the whole world in mind, with the hope of creating a universal beginners' introduction to my teachings at Happy Science. Of all my publications, I believe this is the best preparatory book for new members in Japan, the United States, and elsewhere.

Ryuho Okawa
Founder and CEO
Happy Science Group
January 2011

INTRODUCTION

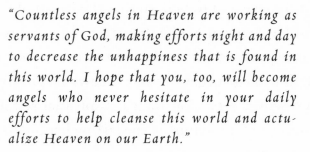

"*Countless angels in Heaven are working as servants of God, making efforts night and day to decrease the unhappiness that is found in this world. I hope that you, too, will become angels who never hesitate in your daily efforts to help cleanse this world and actualize Heaven on our Earth.*"

— Master Ryuho Okawa

The Moment of Truth: Become a Living Angel Today, by Master Ryuho Okawa, reveals the power that resides within all of you, as children of God, to advance your individual characters while bettering the prospects for peace and happiness in the world at large. Master Okawa believes that all of you possess the innate potential to become

God's angels while you live on Earth. All you have to do is awaken to the Truth of your nature: that you are spiritual beings with sacred missions to perform while you exist on Earth.

This book encourages you to explore the spiritual aspects of your life, to see the light of God within you, and to believe that the world of God and Heaven is not a myth but a reality that is far greater and wondrous that you can ever imagine. Within these pages, Master Okawa inspires you to discover a passion for your spiritual self and empowers you to pursue the lasting happiness he describes.

The wisdom in this book is profound and deep, yet decidedly simple. These comprehensive teachings reconcile and harmoniously merge cultural, spiritual, religious, and material beliefs from around the world that have been in a constant state of conflict for thousands of years. Millions of readers and followers across national borders and religious boundaries cherish Master

Okawa's teachings, which are read in many languages today. This is a book for all people of all races on all spiritual and religious paths.

In his homeland of Japan, Master Okawa is a well-known spiritual leader who has delivered more than 1,400 lectures throughout the country. He also travels abroad extensively to bring the words of God to people in all parts of the world; in recent years, he has spoken to audiences in New York, Los Angeles, San Francisco, London, Seoul, Taiwan, Sydney, and São Paulo. People who have seen him speak are amazed by the dignity and power that flow through his presence and his words. Moved by his love and compassion, many people come to see Master Okawa as the voice of Heaven.

He founded the spiritual movement Happy Science in 1986, and between then and April 2011 published over seven hundred books. He has produced an incredible fifty-one store-released books in 2010 alone. His books are now available in nineteen languages, including English, Spanish, Portuguese, Chinese, French, and Korean.

In his most recent travels to Brazil in November 2010, he delivered a week-long series of five lectures in São Paulo, Sorocaba, and Jundiai, which have been compiled into this book. Although the lectures were given to a Brazilian audience, their contents unmistakably appeal to people of all ages, races, and faiths. These talks convey Master Okawa's passion for bringing the path of happiness and the path to Heaven's gate to all people throughout the world.

One of the principal themes in *The Moment of Truth* is Master Okawa's conviction that spiritual happiness is not obtained only when you enter the next life, as some religions teach. Rather, it is something that must be gained during your life on Earth. As a child of God, you have the ability to be a living angel, filled with happiness as you pursue your goal of bringing worldwide peace, everlasting happiness, and prosperity to people on Earth. This sacred mission requires perseverance. But the effort these holy endeavors require is the essence of what gives you everlasting joy, both during this temporary sojourn on Earth and in the next world. This book will guide you through the universal Truths—the Truths of God—that govern your life and the whole world.

In Chapter 1, "Your Path to Happiness," Master Okawa encourages you to be the author of your life. A part of God resides within you. Therefore, you have the power to steer your mind in any direction. You can choose to tap into the light of God within your heart, attune your mind to Heaven, and live for the sake of the greater world's happiness. When you live with the belief that your personal happiness and the happiness of others always go hand in hand, you become a living symbol of God's light.

Chapter 2, "Awaken Your Soul to God's Truths," reveals principles of life that you can practice to confidently steer your mind toward Heaven. You can pave your own path to happiness and save yourself by learning the workings of God and how they affect your mind; once you understand them and learn how to attune your mind to Heaven, the angels will be able to give you much more help. Master Okawa describes the four basic paths that, if followed, will lead to your destination in Heaven. He sums up the paths in four simple words: love, wisdom, self-reflection, and progress. Together, they form a way of life that empowers you to steer your mind toward Heaven even as you navigate life on Earth.

In Chapter 3, "Angels Dispel Darkness and Spread Love," Master Okawa describes how you can develop a lasting happiness that you can bring to the next world without sacrificing your happiness in this life. Many religions teach about God, Heaven, and Hell, but few, if any, teach how you can attain in this world the kind of meaningful happiness that will take you to Heaven. It all depends on the strength of your love and how you counteract the forces of evil as you strive to become living angels and aspire to bring happiness to other people. In this pursuit, you might encounter evils both within you and in the outside world. Master's teachings will help you conquer jealousy and hatred, and awaken the angel inside you. He will give you a strong faith that evil is no match for God and his angels and that you can serve as a force for actualizing Heaven on Earth.

Chapter 4, "Invincible Thinking Can Turn Struggles into Success," introduces Master Okawa's philosophy of invincible thinking. No one is ever immune to the trials and tribulations that life presents. With invincible thinking, however, you can take control of your life. Invincible thinking empowers you to find success within life's defeats and setbacks. This philosophy is not simply about optimism or positive affirmations. Nor is it based on a denial of reality. Rather, invincible thinking is a full and generous acceptance of the obstacles you encounter and the failings that you can never seem to overcome. Invincible thinking enables you to view your problems as God's love in disguise, pointing you to a richer and more fulfilling life. Master Okawa shows you how to take any struggle and turn it into success.

In Chapter 5, "Opening the Door to Miracles," Master Okawa reveals his passionate and heartfelt message, calling on you to awaken your innate faith in God and Heaven. His teachings, the Truths of God, will rouse your soul's memories of the mystical world that surrounds you. As faith in God and Heaven grows in force and spreads all over the world, it will trigger many mystical phenomena that will change the lives of countless people. Today, you could be one of those who experience Heaven's miracles.

Finally, in Chapter 6, "Q&A with Master Okawa," Master fields questions that he has received from his audiences. Topics include whether you can change your fate, the spiritual causes of depression, whether predestination exists, and more. As an expert on the Truths of the soul and the spirit world, he can comprehensively respond to questions that no other religion, including Christianity, could ever answer. He will show you what God's true intentions are. Unlike the fearful and punishing portrayal of God propagated by some religions, the true God is one of infinite love and compassion.

The moment of truth is here, the moment for all of us to awaken our inner angels. This book gives you a glimpse into a powerful spiritual movement that has caught fire in many parts of the world, as people of faith and courage have taken up their sacred callings to help actualize peace, love, and enlightenment on Earth. Within these pages, Master Okawa sends his deepest blessings, the path to your happiness, and the road to Heaven's gate.

> "We humans have the power to change who
> we are, to improve ourselves, and to turn our

future into one of great dreams and ideals. That is what makes us children of God. This is our divine nature."

— Chapter 2, Awaken Your Soul to God's Truths

Chapter One

YOUR PATH TO
HAPPINESS

※

PAVING THE PATH TO HAPPINESS

While on the expressway from São Paulo to our temple in Jundiai, I couldn't help but notice many potholes in the road. The ride was so bumpy and curvy that I actually thought that we were driving on a local road. I was surprised when they told me that we were on the expressway. I also was surprised to see a lot of litter on the streets.

I spent the ride deep in the thought and contemplation that I am this very road, this "path to happiness." I imagined what it feels like and what it means to be a road. I thought, "There are countless cars traveling on my back and a multitude of people walking on me too." Many people litter the road with trash; nevertheless, the road never stops carrying trucks from place to place. Streets are useful and important, yet sometimes they are taken for granted and treated with disrespect. But that is the way things are, sometimes.

When I look over the past, I think about my very first lecture in Tokyo in November 1986, when I spoke to an audience of just over ninety people. Now, twenty-four years later, we have grown and expanded so much that we have built a *shoshinkan*, a main temple, in Brazil, which is literally on the other side of the world. To my joyful realization, I've finally come to the other side of Earth, halfway around the world.

As I've written and spoken about numerous times, my mission is to teach God's Truths, not only to Japan, but also to people everywhere. This sense of mission is renewed within me once again, as I travel around the world. In this spirit, I want to provide you with and remind you of hints for finding happiness.

You Are the Author of Your Life

You, and no one else, can decide your happiness or unhappiness. If you think that you are happy or unhappy based on other people telling you that you are fortunate or unfortunate, then you are mistaken. It is up to you to decide whether you are happy or not. Every day, when you wake up in the morning, tell yourself, "I am the one who decides whether or not today will be filled with happiness. It all depends on me." Keep this thought with you throughout the day. It is you, not anyone else, who makes your day joyful or cheerless.

For example, let's say that the sky is covered with dark clouds and strong winds are moving them quickly. It looks like it may even rain and thunder. You then may think that your day will

3

be ruined because of the weather. But remember that others will say to themselves, "Despite the rain and thunder, I was able to attend a lecture by Master Okawa, who came all the way from Japan. I didn't let the bad weather hinder me from coming to listen to Master."

I have taught many times, through many different words, that you don't have to let the weather or other conditions around you determine how you feel. You possess the power to control your thoughts. If you are a person who is filled with joy, then the environment no longer matters. If you can grasp at least this one point, you will not stray far from the path to happiness.

You are the author of your life. You decide your happiness or unhappiness. It is your mind that chooses one or the other. Please do not forget this Truth. This is one of my key teachings.

Some of you reading this book may be immigrants. You might think that moving to a foreign country can cause your happiness or unhappiness.

But please remember that in the past, many people have immigrated to foreign lands, and each of them seized either happiness or unhappiness with his or her own hands. Each one of them was the creator of his or her life. Everything begins with this point.

It is very easy to blame other people or the environment that surrounds you. And I cannot deny that these things have influence. Bad weather can make you feel glum, and it's hard to find motivation when the economy is doing poorly. It's difficult not to feel disappointed when someone criticizes or disregards you. Nevertheless, it is up to you to decide how you react to these outside influences.

While conventional religions depict a weak image of humanity, I teach a belief in a much stronger form of human being. Each and every one of you possesses much greater resilience than you think. Why do I say this? Because, as many of you probably learned in different religions, including Christianity, God created humans.

5

Since God created humans, a part of God resides in every human being. This is an unwavering fact.

What is God? God is light, and a part of this light resides inside you. So please have more confidence in yourself. The real you is actually much, much stronger than you know. You are brimming with much more potential than you have ever realized. You have great power within to change yourself.

As you strive to change and aim to grow ever closer to God, spirits in Heaven watch over you and guide you from a world beyond this world. You can call them gods. But there are many beings who live close to God, called angels, bodhisattvas, and *tathagatas*. [See Note 1, p. 15] They are Guiding Spirits of Light who are always watching over you. As you discover the light of God within yourself, they celebrate. They say, "You've finally awakened! The moment has finally arrived! You've finally awakened to your true self-worth." Please know that these beings, living in a world that's hidden from your physical eyes, rejoice that you have finally awakened to your mission in life and can begin the work you were meant to accomplish.

I, too, came to Earth from a place in Heaven, far above the surface of this world. I come with one great destiny: to spread the Truths. I believe that my life is not my own. I believe that the entirety of my life, 100 percent of it, is based on God's designs. I strongly believe that I am the very light that shines brightly upon Earth.

A myriad of people will follow on the path I tread on, for my feet will pave the path to their happiness. The many difficulties I have experienced in life do not matter to me because it gives me joy to know that many people will follow the path that I blazed. It brings me great happiness to know that I am making others happy. This is true not only for me, but for every single one of you.

You will never find happiness if you pursue it only for yourself. People who pursue their individual happiness only think about taking love from the people around them and drawing others' love to them. They feel that love has to be seized from others, and that happiness is something others should provide for them. Then, when they find themselves unsatisfied with how much they've seized, when they haven't gained the love and happiness they think they deserve, their dissatisfaction turns into a grudge against society or anger at the whole world. They vent their frustration and discontent on others. For some, their resentment becomes so aggressive that it results in their committing crimes against society and harming the people who live around them.

These people believe that love is something that is supplied by other people. Deep down, they think the people around them have an obligation to make them happy. But that is absolutely not how it should be. We have the duty to bring others happiness. It is our noble duty to love others. And it is because we have a noble duty to give others joy that we not only have the right to find our *own* happiness, but also have the *responsibility* to find it.

The happiest people alive are those who live with the conviction that their individual happiness and the happiness of other people always go hand in hand. Many of these people strive to give love to others through their work. They build their lives on being people who deliver happiness. Those of you who live by this creed shine light onto the world. You are the world's light. This light comes from God, and a part of God's light dwells inside each one of you. Live with a fervent desire to spread happiness to others, and live out your life based on acts of giving love. Within such a life, you will surely see the path of your own happiness open before you.

Even the countries that suffer from poverty and crime today may become the center of the world in the generation of your children or your grandchildren. There are countries in the world that are full of crime and poverty, like Brazil. But these same countries also have a promising future. The United States had a golden age. Japan had a prosperous period. Today, China is rapidly increasing its strength as a superpower. India will be next to rise as a world power, with some economic forecasts predicting that it will outrun China by the year 2050. It is also predicted that Brazil is next in line to emerge as a world power.

I travel around the world not only to speak to you who are presently living. I visit each country to plant seeds of hope for the unborn of future generations, to plant the seeds that will help that country become a beacon of light for the whole world. A future filled with light will surely come. Yes, you might have to face the struggles of poverty, the troubles of a turbulent economy, the grief and trials of illness, or a future that may not permit you onto its path. But you must never forget that the work you do today will become a wondrous gospel for the next generations. You are planting the seeds of hope for the future.

I sincerely hope that all of you will become practitioners of happiness for the sake of the people to come. Please be the living symbols of

God's happiness. To do this, the first thing you must know is that you are the one who is in charge of choosing between happiness and unhappiness.

YOUR SOUL IS THE REAL YOU

I have explored and studied the spirit world for the past thirty years. Although many of my books have yet to be translated into other languages, I have published over six hundred books in Japanese and given more than 1,400 lectures. I have continued to offer new teachings, guiding a multitude of people to the path of happiness. One thing I would like you to know is that the spirit world, which includes both Heaven and Hell, really exists. There is no doubt about this Truth.

When you die, you will go back to the spirit world. But you can only bring your mind, the core part of your soul, to the spirit world. You can take nothing else with you. The material possessions you own on Earth—your house, money, clothes, and even academic achievements and worldly status—are

11

all insubstantial in the face of death. Your spiritual body, which lives inside your physical body, is the "real you." Since a part of God's light is found within each of you, this means that your soul is your true self. Please keep a strong hold on this Truth.

When you go home to the spirit world, you will be assessed on the clarity, pureness, beauty, and richness of your mind. When you walk through the gates of Heaven, you will only have your mind to show. Deepen your belief in and understanding of this Truth as much as you can. Since the mind is the only possession you can take with you to the other world, all of what you experience in this world are materials that help cleanse, buff, and polish your mind. This is the very purpose of life.

None of you will be able to completely avoid difficulties, adversities, setbacks, broken relationships, and events that bring deep sorrow. What is essential is to use these events and experiences to polish your mind and give it a brilliant luster. Some people dwell on the hurt and pain that other people caused them. Some plan their lives around gaining revenge on those who hurt them. But it is a great mistake to live that way. This world is meant to be a place for you to gain all kinds of experiences. It is meant as an opportunity to cultivate a rich, round, and beautiful heart.

FAITH GIVES YOU STRENGTH

You will face moments when you feel lost and don't know which decisions to make. This world is filled with temptations that only add to the confusion. When you feel lost in life and don't know where to turn, always choose faith. Please make the resolution to live for faith alone.

People who choose faith are by no means weak. In fact, by choosing faith, you are proving that you have courage. It takes great courage to believe in something that is completely invisible and to devote your life to values that cannot be perceived by the eyes. People of faith are not weak. They are brave and strong people who are truly loved by God. God expects great things from such people. Please know that, without faith, you will not be able to surmount the wall that stands between this world and the other world.

Nearly thirty years have passed since I started exploring the Truths. I have received many messages from several hundreds of Guiding Spirits living in Heaven. However, everything I have taught in these thirty years is consistent. My teachings have been based on what I have discussed here.

What I have told you in this chapter is the truest form of science. Science is the mind of exploring. It is about the mind that never denies the unknown, and seeks after it. To seek after the unknown is *not* to defy the age of knowledge that we are in today. Instead, I am referring to the science of the future, the science of happiness, the science of the spirit world. It is science that encompasses the mystical.

I hope from my heart that all the countries in the world will go on to make greater progress in the future.

NOTES

1. (Page 6) Heaven is divided into different levels. The higher the dimension, the closer the inhabitants are to God. Bodhisattvas are Divine Spirits who reside in the seventh dimension of Heaven. They are angels of light whose roles are characterized by altruism and selfless acts of compassion toward others. They work hands-on, as servants of God, to bring salvation to people. Tathagatas are Divine Spirits who reside in the eighth dimension of Heaven. Their power and strength of compassion surpass those of bodhisattvas. They primarily focus on expounding teachings based on God's Truths, and leading and providing guidance to other angels and to people on Earth. Tathagatas are beings who have transcended the human condition and sit close to God.

Chapter Two

AWAKEN YOUR SOUL TO
GOD'S TRUTHS

BELIEVING IN THE SPIRIT WORLD IS
THE BEGINNING OF ENLIGHTENMENT

After lecturing at local temples around the world, I ask the audience to fill out questionnaires. I am always pleasantly surprised at how perceptive the audience members are and how many topics for talks I have culled from their responses and questions. I have found that no matter where they live, all humans worry about and seek the same things. To my great pleasure, I can tell from the questionnaire sheets that my teachings have reached the hearts of many and truly have the power to save people.

Regardless of where they live, people must fulfill certain conditions to make them worthy of being part of humanity. The criteria that make humans who they are and compose the standards by which they must live can be summed up as "an awareness of God's Truths." What does "an awareness of God's Truths" mean? On a small scale, it refers to each individual's spiritual awareness about the Truths of the world and who he or she is. It is the process of each person's individual enlightenment. In a broader context, however, it also refers to the first step toward an enlightenment that is common to all humankind. The criteria for awakening to these spiritual, universal Truths, is what I will be talking about in this chapter.

The first step to enlightenment is understanding that a large spirit world exists beyond this world and envelops and encompasses Earth. It is essential for everyone to understand that the true world exists far beyond the one we live in now. Knowledge of this other world brings us to the realization that God also must exist. The world beyond is our true home where we all return after death. From this Truth, people discover that Earth is a place where our souls undergo training or a type of discipline.

These simple and basic Truths are essential for modern human beings to know and understand. All people, no matter where they live on Earth, should be awakened to these spiritual Truths. The world today has grown and greatly advanced since the time of ancient civilizations. Yet, in spite of advancements in the realms of science and technology, people have lost sight of the simplest, yet most essential Truths that we all must live by. We exist in an age when helicopters fly frequently across our skies, but this does not imply that the fundamental Truths of this world have ever changed.

MY ENLIGHTENMENT ABOUT THE SPIRIT WORLD

I started teaching nearly thirty years ago when I received spiritual messages from Heaven through

18

automatic writing. Then, the spirits began using my vocal cords to speak through me. After that, my own enlightenment reached such a high state that I could begin teaching the laws of the universe based on my own level of awareness.

In the year 2010 alone, I delivered over two hundred lectures. My sense of self-identity and sense of duty to fulfill my calling as a religious leader and savior began to take real shape. I ask my disciples to spread the Truths to the ends of the world, but I also have acted on these words by teaching the Truths everywhere. It is my goal to bring salvation to people not only in Japan but also to spread God's Truths to all corners of the world.

In a previous life, 2,500 years ago, I was born as Shakyamuni Buddha in India. As my life of eighty years was about to come to a close, I made the promise to be reborn 2,500 years later to preach the Truths again in an eastern land of Asia. In 1956, exactly 2,500 years after Shakyamuni

Buddha passed into the next world, I was born in Japan. This was a significant year as many countries in Asia celebrated at that time the 2,500-year anniversary of Shakyamuni Buddha's return to Heaven. I kept my promise to be born in Japan and went on to attain enlightenment at twenty-four years of age. Then, at thirty, I began holding activities to create a religious movement that would spread the Truths.

Please remember that I send a part of myself to Earth only once every three thousand years. Thus, the teachings I deliver to people on Earth must last three thousand years. It is with this sense of duty that I deliver the universal Truths, which include the principles that will guide you to the world of happiness. I teach you these Truths and principles in a simple and uncomplicated way, so I can bring enlightenment to as many people as possible.

Many noble Divine Spirits, living in the highest reaches of the spirit world in Heaven, are always seeking to send teachings to people on Earth. They deliver these Truths through a chosen person or persons. Throughout the history of humankind, this is how God's Truths have been taught to people on Earth. It is the same this time. Through my teachings, a vast number of Divine Spirits have revealed their unique messages to you.

I am an expert in the spirit world and in spiritual Truths. As the master of this invisible world, I want to provide you with teachings and principles that will lead to the world of happiness in the afterlife. For this chapter, I have chosen a teaching based on Buddhism. In Chapter 3, I will cover teachings that are similar to Christianity.

The Path to Heaven Starts with Faith

Our happiness or unhappiness in the next life is ultimately decided when we leave this world and return to the other world. The first step to enlightenment is to know that the spirit world does exist, and that your journey back to the original world begins now. The second important point I must tell you is that you must reflect and check whether your life and your way of living thus far has been attuned to Heaven, or directed toward the worlds of Hell. You can examine your life and differentiate between the two on your own.

All people who return to Heaven share clear, common characteristics. First and foremost of these characteristics is correct faith. Those who do not have correct faith have yet to mature fully as human beings, for faith is one of the conditions of being wholly human. Faith is not a quality that animals possess. But we, as members of the human race, and especially those of us who aspire to be noble, must have correct faith.

What is meant by correct faith? The Principles of Happiness which I will speak about are part of this correct faith. These four principles, which I collectively call the Fourfold Path, govern the attainment of human happiness.

The Fourfold Path — Guides to Spiritual Happiness

The Principles of Happiness in the Fourfold Path are love, wisdom, self-reflection, and progress. The first principle is love.

LOVE

People tend to covet love. They seek love for themselves from others. This, however, will not lead you to Heaven. Instead, to return to Heaven, you must not take love, but do the exact opposite. You must be a giver of love. The path to Heaven is found by giving your love without any considerations or expectations of personal gains or losses. In this way, we can love our brothers and sisters who are living with us now on Earth. So, what does it mean to love?

To love is
To recognize the beauty in other people.

To love is
To recognize that others have
The right to find happiness, too.

To love means
To encourage others to live splendid lives,
And not to focus only on your own life.

To love is
To feel joy when you see someone else.
Find happiness, become affluent.
Or enter the right path.

This is the Principle of Love.

WISDOM

The second principle is wisdom. The Principle of
Wisdom today encompasses gaining an under-

standing of the diverse worldviews that exist in our modern era. But the most essential and foundational part of this principle is the knowledge that will raise your awareness and understanding of the relationship between this world and the other. Wisdom is about gaining a proper life perspective, an accurate spiritual knowledge of the meaning of life, which is the only possession you can bring with you to the other world upon your death.

That's why you must live with a spiritual view of life. This is what this principle indicates. Everyone has material things to do every day to continue making a living in this world. We have jobs, a family to care for, and many other obligations that keep us busy. Yet, we should not let ourselves become wholly consumed by the bustling details of our lives. We must remember that we are spiritual beings, and that without fail, the time will come for all of us to leave this world and journey on to the next one.

You can live with a spiritual view of life by looking at your state of being in the way God would see it through His eyes. Check every day to see whether God would approve your way of life. The Principle of Wisdom is about the power that comes when you are rooted in the daily practice of examining your life.

It is also about the power you gain as you turn the experiences and knowledge you have acquired thus far into wisdom for living a wondrous life on Earth. You could find clues to this wisdom in the words of Divine Spirits in Heaven who have spoken through me in their spiritual messages. You also might grasp clues in my lectures about how you can live a better life. In essence, the Principle of Wisdom is about trying to live with the eyes of God as your own and leading a life He would approve.

SELF-REFLECTION

The third principle is the Principle of Self-Reflection. I have found that, for the most part, Christian doctrines do not offer in-depth teaching about self-reflection. Catholic churches offer confessionals, where you have a chance to confess your sins and seek God's forgiveness. By contrast, I teach that we have the ability within ourselves to reflect on our thoughts and deeds. I teach that we have the power to determine on our own whether our thoughts and deeds are proper or wrong in light of the Truths.

The purpose of this practice of self-reflection is not simply to condemn yourself about every mistake and error you've made. The true purpose of self-reflection is the attainment of happiness. By this, I mean that everything you experience in life, including all the thoughts you've ever had and all the things you have ever done, are recorded in your mind.

When you leave this world and travel to the other world, your life will be shown to you much like a film in a movie theater. Many of your close family members and friends will be watching the film with you. Your mentors, parents, friends, and former teachers will come to watch this film about your life, condensed into about an hour or two. They will view this movie with you to help you determine the success of your life, or the lack thereof. When you finish watching your life movie, you will be able to judge for yourself. Observing the reactions of the rest of the audience will also help you judge whether your life was right or wrong, a success or a failure. You will then choose for yourself whether you will go to Heaven or Hell. You will choose the course that is most appropriate for you.

There are many paths in Heaven, but there are many paths in Hell as well. You will go to the place that offers the soul training that is right for you. For example, those who kill, hurt, and cause many people harm will need to take the path of self-reflection in the next life. They will go to a realm where others like them exist. They will find themselves living with others who, for example, shot and killed many people. As they live amongst such people, they will begin to see their own reflections within others, as if they were looking into a mirror. They will look at other people who are just like them and begin to see the ugliness within them reflected back.

So, after our death, we will head to a world that represents the characteristic that is strongest within our souls. There, we will join other souls with the same tendencies. This is why I ask you to study God's Truths and to practice self-reflection while you are still living in this world. That is why the practice of self-reflection is, in fact, a principle of salvation.

You have the power to save yourself, if you only take the time to learn God's Truths and use that knowledge to reflect on your life. If you do this within your sojourn on Earth, you might not have to do it in the other world. If you make these efforts, the angels, bodhisattvas, and tath-agatas in Heaven will extend their helping hands to you. The congregations of spirits in Heaven are there to help people who are persevering in changing themselves, and these spirits will surely shine their light on you.

Please know that instant salvation rarely occurs. Salvation always requires effort on your part. You have to become aware of your own errors to find true salvation. Many religions simplify their teachings and make salvation seem easy so that they can spread their teachings farther and with less effort. However, it is very important that individuals attain as much enlightenment as possible about their true divine nature and determine for themselves how they ought to live in light of this inner divinity. This is the teaching of self-reflection, and it bestows onto you the power to save yourself.

As you practice self-reflection, the mistakes you made and the sins you've committed thus far will be erased. A simple belief in Jesus will not be sufficient to forgive or erase your sins. They will be erased when you realize the mistakes you've made and spend time reflecting on them and repenting for them. Self-reflection will change those errors that have been recorded in your mind.

Then, when you watch that film of your life

in the next world and the audience sees scenes of you self-reflecting each time you make mistakes, the spirits in the audience will be thrilled. You will hear a rush of applause resounding through the theater. They will congratulate you with a sigh of relief. This is the Principle of Self-Reflection.

PROGRESS

The last principle is the Principle of Progress. This principle teaches us not to keep our enlightenment or our happiness to ourselves. Instead, we should make efforts to spread that happiness to the rest of society, the country, and other parts of the world. This principle encourages us to foster positive and constructive dreams and thoughts and do what we can to create a Utopia on Earth.

If you live by these four principles, you will be on your way to Heaven in the afterlife. This is not about finding salvation from an external power or source. You will find your way to Heaven through the efforts you make on your own. Please hold these four principles close to your heart as you go through life. Never forget to live with the eyes of God as your own, and remember that you will eventually journey on to the next life.

We humans have the power to change who we are, improve ourselves, and turn our future into one of great dreams and ideals. That is what makes us children of God. This is our divine nature. You might find fragments of evil or dark clouds that loom within your mind. But deep within you resides your awareness as a child of God. So awaken it, and discover the power within you to save yourself. It is my duty to tell you this.

By attaining this form of enlightenment, people have managed to get rid of the evil spirits that have been possessing them. Many people have seen their illnesses cured. I am not curing these illnesses, nor am I getting rid of the evil spirits. You can chase away these fragments of evil all on your own by making your mind shine brightly.

In this chapter, I have spoken to you about

my fundamental teachings: the exploration of the Right Mind and the method of putting this exploration into practice, as well as the Fourfold Path of love, wisdom, self-reflection, and progress. These are my teachings in a nutshell, the very basics of the wisdom I am trying to spread. In that sense, what I covered here is fundamental, unmistakably valuable, and universal to all people on Earth. Seek to deepen your understanding of these teachings, and share them with others.

Chapter Three

ANGELS DISPEL
DARKNESS AND
SPREAD LOVE

HEAVEN'S LIGHT
SPREADS TO THE WORLD

I would like to talk to you all about the theme of love. Specifically, I want to talk about the mind of God and the minds of angels as seen from the perspective of Heaven, not from the perspective of this world. I hope this will give you a glimpse of the true minds of God and the angels. I approached this theme in 1987, at the age of thirty-two, when I gave my second public lecture before seven thousand people. The lecture was titled "The Principle of Love." I recently watched that lecture again and realized how much of what I talked about two decades ago has come true today.

I foretold very clearly what would happen in the future. I said that in ten to twenty years, our movement to create Utopia in this world would reach beyond countries and spread throughout the world, and that this movement would grow beyond a religious philosophy and become a giant surge that would change many aspects of society. Just as I had foreseen, I now am acting upon my own words to spread these teachings to the ends of the world. I travel across the ocean and around the world to give lectures.

I have dedicated myself to spreading God's Truths. I know this sounds extreme. But I would not hesitate to die for the sake of the Truths. I continue my efforts every day and live each day to the fullest, so I know I could die without any regrets even if today turned out to be the last day of my life.

I serve as a voice, a mouthpiece, for Heaven's light, wisdom, and love. I can only descend to Earth once every few millenniums. So I do not want to take this opportunity for granted. I want to spread the words of Truths to as many people as I can.

Two, three, four thousand years ago, when the transportation system was still undeveloped, it was difficult to spread the Truths. However, today, we can fly to the ends of the Earth in hours. Our communication systems dispatch messages around the world in seconds. We are very lucky to be living in such an era, for the Truth can now touch more people than ever before.

Japan may seem like a tiny island hiding in a corner of the world map. It may be very, very difficult to believe in teachings that come from such a small island. Although I have had more than six hundred books published in Japanese—fifty-one books in the year 2010 alone—only twenty-seven of my books have been published in English. It takes a great amount of time for the teachings to reach you because of the language barrier. Currently, groups of people who have embraced my teachings can be found in more than eighty countries. I am truly grateful that you have, from the few teachings available, grasped the essence of the Truths I have delivered thus far, and that you have entered the path of faith.

My home country, Japan, has made great progress in many fields, including technology, economics, mass media, and politics. Unfortunately, however, Japan has fallen behind in a religious sense, and many people today live without faith. Other countries may regard religion highly, but sometimes the religions that are found in these countries are still imperfect. Most faiths are unable to provide true and lasting happiness to people. I believe that the issue behind this is a misunderstanding of love.

DISSOLVING JEALOUSY, THE ROOT OF HATRED

Do you know what the opposite of love is? It is not hatred, as most people might suspect. The opposite of love is jealousy. Many people across the world struggle with this issue. It is usually jealousy, not hatred, that breaks apart friends, families, and relationships. Jealousy has its roots in something very fundamental, and it has dangerous aspects and disgraceful characteristics.

When you harbor jealousy, it is not directed indiscriminately toward just anyone. The only people who spark jealousy within you are those who are highly skilled in your area of interest. For example, if you dream of becoming a professional soccer player some day, you might feel jealous of people who are more talented at playing soccer than you are. In contrast, you probably wouldn't harbor jealousy toward a wrestler. If you strongly desire wealth, you might become jealous of the rich and prosperous. If you want to be in a romantic relationship, you would feel jealous of people who are popular among the opposite gender.

To overcome jealousy, the first step you must take is to understand that jealousy—the complete opposite of love—is a part of your mind's mechanism that tries to destroy your ideals and the ideal image of yourself. Deep within your heart, in your subconscious, you aim to be like the person that has sparked jealousy within you; that person is or has what you desire.

The problem is that when your jealousy arises, it actually works to stop you from moving closer to your goal. This happens when you criticize, put down, and point out the shortcomings of those who have provoked your jealousy. It is very important for you to be honest with yourself and acknowledge your desire to be like the person who has incited your jealousy. This acknowledgement will help quiet your feelings. Once your jealousy is subdued, bless that person instead.

A heart that blesses is a heart that affirms or recognizes the good in others. It is a heart that aspires to reach an ideal and wishes for other people's happiness. As long as you have this mindset, your life will be gradually guided toward the ideal that you are pursuing. For example, let's say you are someone who is passionate about your studies. You might struggle with feelings of jealousy toward someone who is very adept as a student. But you mustn't be blatant about it and criticize him or her. Instead, praise that person's efforts. When you can do this, you will be one or even two steps closer to obtaining what the other person possesses. Please remember that jealousy is a roadblock to your dreams and will deny you your ideals.

People commonly feel jealousy toward those with wealth. Even in countries whose urban areas are seemingly making great leaps in their growth and progress, large disparities between economic classes remain major issues. Many people are still living in poverty, a problem that governments have difficulty solving. It is a very challenging problem to tackle. When jealousy toward those with wealth grows, it changes into hatred. When the feeling of hatred expands further, it becomes aggression and leads to an increase in crime.

Antisocial conduct and aggressive actions against society only destroy your dreams and ideals. They only close off your path to self-realization.

If you wish to be friends with the wealthy, you must have a heart that blesses them. Affluent people will open their hearts to you if you congratulate them and show that you wish to be like them. This is how the wealthy become friends with the poor and teach the poor how to become successful in business. People want to become friends with those who bless them. If you aspire to make this world a better place, you must carefully nurture a heart that desires to increase the number of happy people, not the number of unhappy people. Please remember this.

THE FIRST FALLEN ANGEL

A long time ago, Lucifer was one of the seven archangels. Originally, he was called the "angel of wisdom," "son of the dawn," or "son of daybreak." But after

THE MOMENT OF TRUTH

his death, he journeyed into Hell and became Satan. Lucifer's jealousy of God caused his fall. Originally, Lucifer was a beautiful, shining angel who was full of wisdom. However, he couldn't stand the fact that he could not become God, and he was unable to contain his jealousy. When he was born onto Earth under the name Satan, he lived with a heart filled with greed for power, a craving for worldly desires, and a thirst for dominance. Dark clouds filled his heart as he continued in his aggressive behavior, and he could not return to Heaven. Lucifer, the first ever fallen angel, was the product of jealousy.

God was Lucifer's ideal. He wanted to be someone exactly like God. Lucifer should have controlled his jealousy of God. He should have tried to imitate God's characteristics, actions, and heart. Lucifer should have fashioned his ideal self in this way and changed himself into God's likeness. But his jealousy interfered and caused his fall to Hell. When Lucifer fell to Hell, many others suffered with him. Back then, a shallow

Hell was already developing, formed by souls who had committed evil while they were alive. Then, when Lucifer became Satan, a devil in Hell, he began to wage war upon Heaven.

The war he waged was this; he discovered that he could not influence any of the souls who lived in Heaven. However, he realized that the vibrations of people living on Earth were closer to those found in Hell than to those in Heaven. So whenever he found people in this world who resonated with the vibrations in Hell, he sent evil spirits to possess them. These spirits would lure the living into a destructive way of life, and, ultimately, pull these people right into Hell at their death. This is how he has been steadily increasing the population of souls in Hell.

Hell is a dark, merciless, and excruciating place. There is nothing positive or wonderful about it. To escape the pain and suffering even for a little while, spirits in Hell come into this world to possess people who harbor anger, hatred, and jealousy. They possess people who have the same tendencies they do, and while they are possessing them, these spirits are capable of experiencing what it feels to be alive. For that purpose, they enter the world and possess living people, consequently ruining these people's lives.

CONQUERING YOUR NEGATIVE ENERGY

All of you have felt some form of delight, even if it was only slight, at someone else's misfortune. No one can say that they have never smiled inwardly or felt relief at seeing someone fail or fall into hardship. Evil spirits seize upon these moments. These moments attract them and allow them to form connections with you. Your delight in other people's failures or misfortunes becomes the anchor onto which evil spirits can hook their rope ladder and climb out of Hell. They will become attached to you and may begin to cause various illnesses. They might make your relationships fall apart, drag your job or business into disaster, or mislead you and bring your life toward ruin. They also will disrupt your family life and create discord within the home.

These events begin with the jealousy you feel toward others. This downward spiral starts with a heart that finds pleasure in others' misfortunes. It starts with a heart that feels that someone else's mishaps somehow reduce your own state of misery. These pathetic thoughts invite evil spirits to you. But, in fact, it's not very difficult to cut and get rid of the rope ladder that they have hooked onto you. All you need is compassion and sympathy toward those who have failed. All that is necessary is a true desire to help them. When you see others succeed or find happiness, share in their joy and delight. Evil spirits will not be capable of troubling you when you have that kind of mind.

When you are possessed, your body will feel heavy, and you will always feel under the weather. Should you be constantly possessed by evil spirits, this state of depression will continue, and everything in life will look bleak and gray. You will think your future is dark. You will believe nothing good can come your way. Both good and bad happen in every person's life. But you will react violently to negative events and respond less and less to positive things. Somehow, you must break out of this vicious cycle. Do not let your heart attune to devils in Hell. Direct your heart instead toward God. Always attune your heart to the work of angels.

ANGELS ARE BY YOUR SIDE

Even among people who have faith, the number of people who have actually seen God or angels are few. Angels are always working, night and day, to help many, many people. They help people who struggle under the possession of evil spirits. They try to teach them how to fill their hearts with goodness and guide them away from evil. They try to help them encounter people who can guide them toward right faith.

Angels are working like this every day without rest. But you probably cannot see these angels. Because you cannot see them, they do not receive your thanks for the work they do every day to try to save you. The good-will with which they envelop you gets passed by unnoticed.

Occasionally, you might see an angel in your dreams, or perhaps hear a voice that might be an angel's. Moments like this can come to you when you undergo religious discipline. But 99 percent of the time, the daily work of angels goes on unappreciated. So please, give gratitude to God and His angels through your faith.

DEVILS ARE NO MATCH FOR GOD

Hell does exist and the devils continue to wage their war on God. But the devils' domain can only extend to this world. People tend to think of Heaven and Hell, God and the devils, as dichotomies. They see them as being equal opposing forces. But as I mentioned in the books *The Laws of the Sun* and *The Laws of Eternity*, that is not so.

Heaven and Hell are not equal worlds. In the other world, Heaven is an overwhelmingly larger place than Hell. Hell is only a small part of the spirit world. It is only connected to the evil in this physical world. If I compare it to a river, Hell is the mouth of a river where fresh water mixes with sea water, whereas Heaven occupies the upper reaches of the river. An overwhelming difference exists in the power and force between them. Please never forget this.

No devil can defy God. Have strong faith in this Truth. God and the devils are not equal. No devil can ever defeat God because God is light— an overwhelming abundance of light.

Darkness can never conquer light. Darkness itself has no real existence. Darkness only exists in places where light does not shine. When light shines, darkness disappears.

If you believe that darkness really exists, you are mistaken. Your eyes are being deceived. If a place is dark, it is only because something is obstructing the light. To eliminate the darkness and let the light shine, all you need to do is remove the obstruction. The discipline of removing the obstruction is called faith. It is religious discipline and it requires diligent effort.

No evil can subdue the light of God. No evil in this world can defeat light. Take the light of the sun, for example. It is incredibly powerful. Nothing can overpower it. Yes, you could shield the sunlight and create a shadow. You can create a shadow just by holding out your hand. Even a thin piece of paper can shade the sun. But the shadow is never a match against the sunlight. Knowing this will give you courage, a courage based on faith. Remember that no devil can ever challenge God and win against Him.

BECOME AN ANGEL OF LOVE

To save the seven billion people on Earth, God has countless angels working constantly, every day, on His behalf. Angels work day and night without rest. Spirits in Heaven do not sleep. It is only in this world that the day is divided into night and day. There is no night in Heaven.

Countless angels work twenty-four hours a day, 365 days a year, to decrease unhappiness and suffering in this world. They try to comfort those who are in sorrow. But God's angels also serve in another capacity: they provide tough guidance to those who drag others into darkness and cause unhappiness.

The angels are God's emissaries of love. But love is not just about being kind all the time. Kindness is love in its most basic form. However, correcting those who are wrong is also love. Justice is a manifestation of God's love.

God's love can take many forms on Earth. Strong, wise leaders can serve as messengers of love, even if their words may be stern sometimes. But these words are meant to direct you away from the path of evil and sorrow, and toward the path of good and happiness. The wisdom and guidance of good leaders can be another form of love.

In the beginning, I said that the opposite of love is not hatred but jealousy. Jealousy was the reason why the one-time archangel Lucifer fell to Hell. Jealousy, therefore, was the reason Hell expanded. Jealousy can grow easily into hatred and loathing and visibly manifest as destructive acts of evil against others. But remember this: A disciple asked Jesus, "Lord, how many times should I forgive? Up to seven times?" Jesus responded, "Not seven times, but up to seventy times seven." That is what Jesus said. He said to forgive 490 times.

You may have people you loathe. You may have people you hate. But have you ever forgiven them 490 times? Probably not. I will tell you that you must do much more than that. Give love when you are met with hatred. Sweep away hatred with a great river of love. Let the overwhelming force of your goodwill and love overpower the little streams of hatred, anger, and jealousy that try to creep in. This is a condition each country must fulfill to create a future filled with hope.

True love brings hope.
True hope brings glory.
True glory brings you true freedom.
True freedom fully teaches you what is Truth.

Become children of Truth.
Become children of hope.
Become children of prosperity.
Become children of good.

And above all else, become children of God.
This is my strong and earnest hope.

What is the path that you must seek as children of God? Become one of those angels who never hesitate in their daily efforts to help cleanse this world and turn it into a Utopia. I have traveled thousands of miles to give lectures around the world. I keep giving talks because I want you all to become angels. I want you to do the same work that angels are doing, here on Earth. The work you do here on Earth will have ten times more worth than if it was done in the spirit world.

You cannot see Heaven.
You cannot see God.
You cannot see Hell.

But those of you who keep walking on the path to God and the invisible world of Heaven with only faith as your guide are the very people who will become angels. I will pray with all my heart that you will continue to refine your wisdom and make diligent efforts every day toward this goal.

Chapter Four

INVINCIBLE THINKING CAN TURN STRUGGLES INTO SUCCESS

———————— ✳ ————————

THE SUCCESS OF HAPPY SCIENCE

In November 2010, the *Diamond Weekly*, a highly regarded Japanese economics magazine, published a large special feature article about new religions in Japan. More than half of it focused on Happy Science. According to the article, Happy Science has ranked as the number one religion in Japan for two consecutive years, both 2009 and 2010. The magazine provided an extremely detailed analysis of Happy Science and carefully researched it from numerous points of view.

Several other new Japanese religions have succeeded abroad, but in Japan, Happy Science surpasses them in size by fifteen times, according to the *Diamond Weekly*. The magazine states that we have attracted eleven million members in Japan and another one million overseas. We actually have more members than that. But the magazine makes the point that Happy Science is very powerful and receives a great deal of attention in its homeland. More than 80 percent of the Japanese population is familiar with Happy Science and its activities. If you were to ask in Japan who Ryuho Okawa is, almost every person would know. Now I have started traveling all around the world to meet new people. So my teachings are also spreading internationally at a rapid pace.

Happy Science is also the most opinionated of all religions in Japan. We have voiced strong and clear views about governmental issues, politics, economics, and the ideal state of the world.

No other religion has expressed opinions on modern issues of society as firmly as we have. At the same time, however, Happy Science is very well known for the depth and profoundness of its spirituality.

We may face criticisms in the future, but the truth is that we have accomplished much in just a quarter of a century. Society is now acknowledging these accomplishments. One of my very first books continues to be read long after I wrote it, and is read in many languages. *The Laws of Eternity* is a book that I wrote before Happy Science firmly established itself as a religion and before it attracted many members. Now, that book has been translated into Portuguese and other languages. It has even been made into a film that has become quite a hit.

Combined with *The Laws of the Sun* and *The Golden Laws*, *The Laws of Eternity* is a part of the key trilogy, the three basic doctrines of Happy Science, which I wrote when I was thirty years old and was first starting Happy Science. These books, which are now offered in many languages, form the basic framework of my teachings and of Happy Science as a whole. Although I authored them two decades ago, their content is still relevant today.

The book *Invincible Thinking* established our work on a national level. I wrote it when I was thirty-two years old and the organization had been in existence for a little over two years. The book is a compilation of four seminars that I conducted weekly in front of about one thousand people. In its first year of publication, it sold more than two million copies in Japan. It ranked on the bestsellers list of a major newspaper. Until then, the public had tended to distance itself from religious books. However, once the newspaper published a review, the book acquired renown in Japan.

This book has proved to be quite powerful. Internationally, people have overcome differences in religion, philosophy, and creed to read and study many of my books, which makes me truly happy. In the case of *Invincible Thinking,* even countries that are generally atheist or materialistic, where people do not especially believe in God, have accepted it. For instance, the Chinese translation has been well received and many followers in China are studying the book.

BELIEF IN THE SOUL GIVES YOU INVINCIBLE THINKING

Invincible thinking is not about simply affirming an optimistic perspective all the time. On the other hand, it does not subscribe to the very negative view of humanity that is often embodied in the Christian belief of "original sin." Although this may trouble people of the Catholic faith who believe that humans are born with sin, invincible thinking is based on a different philosophy.

Invincible thinking believes that we are souls that dwell in human bodies. The three-dimensional world in which you currently live is not the real world. The real world consists of the higher-dimensional realms of Heaven, beginning with the fourth dimension and continuing upward to the ninth. In essence, you are a soul that inhabited the spirit world and currently lives on Earth.

It is very easy to say that you disbelieve in the existence of the spirit world. But remember, no one, not a single person in the history of humankind, has ever successfully disproved its existence. On the other hand, you will find that countless people have tried to show and explain the other world. A great number of religious leaders, philosophers, thinkers, and moralists in all eras have spoken of the other world and our souls. These people deserve our attention and respect. It is unfair to ignore their efforts and endeavors simply because you decided not to believe in the spirit world. Please acknowledge the work they have left behind, and lend your ears to their words.

Many people around the world believe in the spirit world or have developed theories about

it. The Frenchman Allan Kardec's *The Spirits'
Book* is very popular in Brazil. So is Chico Xavier,
a spiritual medium who passed away a few years
ago. He was known for his abilities in automatic writing, hearing the voices of spirits, and
contacting a spirit named Emmanuel who was
likely his guardian spirit. The movie based on his
life is well known.

When I visited Brazil in November 2010, I
talked to the spirit of Xavier, but it's only been
eight years since he passed away, and he did not
seem to have a full understanding of the spirit
world yet. I purchased his books, called his spirit
in the presence of a number of my staff, and
tried talking to him. Although he is not yet at the
level of enlightenment he is supposed to reach,
I found that he was originally from the realm of
bodhisattvas in the seventh dimension.

He is presently in the stage of trying to understand the other world and sorting out his thoughts.
I spoke to him in an ancient dialect of the region

of Damascus, an area near ancient Rome, and tried hard to help him understand reincarnation, but he appeared to struggle with the concept of it, even though he is a spirit now. Though he responded in the same language, he didn't seem to fully grasp the idea. I think he still needs some time to study.

Many people like him around the world have served to relay the words of people from the other world. I am one of these people; I earnestly publicize the messages of many spirits. For many years, I have continued to prove the existence of the spirit world and Divine Spirits through the publication of numerous spiritual messages. In the year 2010 alone, I published over fifty-one books that have been publicly sold in bookstores. Of those, forty-two are spiritual messages from ninety-three different spirits, published for the purpose of proving the existence of the other world. They are the words and messages of Divine Spirits in Heaven and a few from Hell, including Satan.

Their messages differ from one another in content. Each of the messages is unique, which shows that each comes from a different personality. This is how I am proving that the spirit world does exist. Many years ago, I stopped because the variety and differences found in the messages made my teachings confusing and difficult to understand. I turned my focus to publishing theoretical books of my own teachings based on my own thinking. With the passage of time, however, the number of people who do not believe in the spirit world has risen again. So I have set out once more to publish new spiritual messages.

THIS WORLD IS A SCHOOL FOR YOUR SOUL

If you think that the physical world is the true world, it is easy to judge between happiness and unhappiness. However, if you know that your life is not limited to this world and that you will eventually return to the spirit world that lies beyond this one, then you know that the whole purpose of our lives on Earth is soul training. As the world changes and new eras arrive and pass, you are born time and again with a different name, nationality, occupation, and gender so you can gain new experiences each time. In living as a completely new person, you are furthering your soul's growth. This is the starting point of what constitutes your life.

If you accept the idea that the other world exists and that people return to that world after they die, then you can perceive this world as a school for your soul and understand that everything you experience is allowed to exist for the purpose of your education. If you think in this way, then you must not make the mistake of blaming your parents or the company that employs you for any unfortunate circumstances in which you find yourself.

Yes, outside influences have an impact on your life. The economy fluctuates greatly, and various social changes occur. The presidents of countries can make mistakes in governance and cause misfortune or, if you luck out, spark a recovery. Outside influences are ever present. However, no matter what the times may be, you must not forget that you are the only one who can guide your own mind.

Never forget that no matter how turbulent the currents of the river of fate may become, you are at the helm, steering your ship. You can make mistakes at work. You can make mistakes in love. You can fall ill or fail at an exam. In response to the many things that can happen, you can give in to despair, fall into self-destructive behavior, and fail to believe in yourself and others. You can lose your will to do anything and feel that your future holds nothing but darkness. However, you must firmly maintain the belief that you alone are responsible for viewing your life in that way.

DON'T BLAME OTHERS
FOR YOUR UNHAPPINESS

Some religions blame misfortunes on people's ancestors or evil spirits. If you attribute the cause of your misfortune to "original sin," that is, the sins committed by your far-distant ancestors, then you will not be saved any time soon. The concept of original sin does have its merits. It can be helpful in building up faith or encouraging people to reflect on their mistakes and repent. However, original sin alone is not enough to explain everything about who you are today.

Some people say that the reason you are miserable now is because your ancestors are lost and suffering. In some cases, they are right. Indeed, I have seen numerous cases in which the ancestor is suffering in Hell and possesses the person.

For example, it is true that the phenomenon of ancestors causing their descendents to suffer exists. If you have a strong grudge against someone, then you could find yourself attuned to an ancestor in Hell who also has strong grudges or hatred. Under these circumstances, this ancestor would be able to possess you indefinitely. He or she could make you fall sick, stop your business from succeeding, or cause you to make wrong judgments.

However, I would like to emphasize that the most important thing you can do to determine the course of your life is correct your mind. The law of the spirit world states that spiritual vibrations of the same type attract one another. An evil spirit can possess people on Earth because those people have thoughts similar to those of the evil spirit. It can possess them because their vibrations are at the same level; the thoughts in their minds are the same. If people ceased having evil thoughts, evil spirits couldn't possess them. The way to rid yourself of these influences is to change your frame of mind.

A GOLDEN MIND
CAN ATTUNE TO HEAVEN

It is possible for an outside power to save you, but each individual also can save himself or herself from evil spirits by polishing his or her mind until it shines with light. You can rid yourself of evil influences by cleansing and scrubbing your mind until it sparkles. This is what I would like all of you to know.

When your mind begins to shine after you practice self-reflection and refinement, spiritual light will shine from the back of your head. This is popularly called your aura. Saints are often depicted in paintings with golden halos around their heads. This golden aura actually appears when you are in this state and makes it difficult for evil spirits to possess you. When you can emit light like this, you will connect with Heaven and become attuned to it.

At this stage, you will be able to receive light from your guardian spirit, or even from Guiding Spirits and angels who are higher than your guardian spirit. The light you receive from them is very warm. You will feel any heaviness, pain, and fatigue quickly taken away.

SETBACKS ARE SEEDS OF SUCCESS

Now, what is the essence of invincible thinking? It is to know that this world is a school for your life-long education. It is to know that your most valuable experience is to generate a positive result not only from your successes, but also, and perhaps especially, from your failures. You cannot underestimate the importance of seeing everything as a seed of something positive for the future.

If you succeed, then celebrate it. Be happy. Congratulate yourself for achieving success and for the efforts you put into attaining that success. But instead of becoming full of yourself, it is important to share the joy with others. You must also continually work at building humility so you do not fall into the trap of making mistakes due to conceit. If you suffer a failure, know that hidden

68

within it is the next seed of success. Accept it as the will of the Heavens, the Will of God, and try to understand what you should learn from this experience. It is very important to find the lesson in your failures.

A positive mindset also can help you build a stronger self. For example, I now fly around the world to give talks to audiences in different countries. This is physically straining. Sometimes, I speak even if I feel jet-lagged, or if my talk is scheduled at the very early hours of dawn in the Japanese time zone, or even if I must pull an all-nighter to do so. Traveling around the world taxes me physically. But I do it because I want to meet with as many of you as I can! Overcoming your struggles and difficulties without making excuses is the path to being victorious in life.

Defeat does not exist for someone who lives life in this way. A proactive and positive mindset about any situation will enrich your life and help you onto the path to success. If you live with an attitude of turning everything you encounter into material to refine yourself and into a seed of self-growth, then the very path you walk will be none other than the path to success.

Chapter Five

OPENING THE DOOR TO
MIRACLES

※

A WAVE OF MIRACLES

Christian nations around the world are probably more accepting of spirituality and mystical beliefs than my home country, Japan, is. But many Christians might be skeptical when I say that Jesus Christ is my friend. To be more exact, I guided him from Heaven when he was on Earth two thousand years ago. I sent him all sorts of inspirations and directions. Now, since I am the one who is on Earth, Jesus Christ is sending me many inspirations. Therefore, Catholics would find a philosophical affinity with my teachings.

Jesus Christ's teachings make up almost 30 percent of the entire structure of Happy Science's teachings. Although we also have ideas that are not Christian, Happy Science and Christianity have much in common. We share the teaching of love, and recently, many miracles have occurred in Japan that have been similar to Jesus Christ's miracles. For instance: a cancer was cured; a skull crushed in a traffic accident was restored to its former state without surgery; and a tumor that needed surgical removal disappeared after the person asked me a question and heard my answer in a Q&A session.

The causes of illnesses can originate in this world. But sometimes an illness stems from a person's past life. When this cause is identified through a reading, an illness can vanish the moment the individual acknowledges the past life as its source. The illness disappears because the root cause is no longer there.

In the summer of 2010, when I went to our temple in Hakone, a resort area in Japan, a young man told me that he suspected that he had been an alien in a previous life. He asked me to see if his suspicion was correct. It took me about thirty seconds to conduct a past life reading of him. From that, I uncovered that he indeed had been an extraterrestrial in the past. I told him that he had been a Martian, and that he had dwelled underground. I told him that during that life, he had been a mole about a meter long or some other animal that had lived underground. Yet, even though he had been this subterranean creature, he had possessed the intelligence level of a human being.

Sometime after the reading, I learned that this person had been suffering from a skin allergy condition called atopic dermatitis. He had the disease all over his body, and he was particularly sensitive to sunlight. Exposure to the sun would chap his skin and turn it very, very dry. After I told him that he had been born on Mars in the past, and that he had been a ground-dweller that didn't surface very often, his illness went away. His skin became smooth and problem-free, and the sun no longer bothered him. All it took was just a few words. Episodes like these are happening. In the year 2010 alone, numerous intractable diseases have been cured.

Happy Science's teachings also are spreading in developing countries such as India. There, children don't have the money to go to the hospital or buy medicine. At a school in India that Happy Science funds, about three hundred students practice a prayer I created called "El Cantare Healing." They do it because it will heal illnesses without costing anyone a penny. I saw a video of the children in India practicing the prayer in the school yard. It would be quite difficult for that to happen in Japan.

I will continue to travel to many countries around the world to give talks. If I could, I would like to return to the countries I have visited many more times, but I can never be sure that there will be a next time. With those of you who are not young, that one time I see you may in fact be our first and last meeting. So I feel that I should not pass up any opportunity to speak to you.

FAITH BRINGS MIRACLES

Many mystical things exist in this world. Certain triggers can open the doors to the mystical world. It is important for us to encounter mystical phenomena that we would otherwise never experience or feel in everyday life. Events that seemingly cannot happen within the ordinary laws and principles of our lives really do occur.

For a long time, Happy Science did not discuss the topic of faith. Originally, we started off as a study group. Because we held the stance that we were "researchers" in the science of understanding happiness and in the exploration of the spiritual world, many of our members tended to be very rational and intellectual people. From this perspective, we intentionally obstructed miracles. However, we have come to a point where we cannot stop them anymore. Countless miracles are occurring now. They are spreading beyond the borders of Japan and taking place in places such as the Philippines and Africa. People with illnesses that doctors have given up on treating are finding themselves cured. From now on, many miracles will occur in the countries that I have visited. This is a prophecy, and I foresee that this will happen for a fact.

Events that should not happen in this world but do anyway are called miracles. The trigger that causes these miracles can be summed up in one word—faith. Although miracles may seem like coincidences that should not actually happen, in fact, they are proof of God's salvation. These exceptions occur for the sake of providing hard evidence of God. I believe that many of you will experience miracles and become living proof that you are here on Earth as envoys of God. God will bestow many miracles on you.

According to the Christian Bible, many of the people who later became Jesus Christ's disciples didn't believe in him at first, and they betrayed him. These disciples eventually found faith in Jesus through his miracles. As the disciples came to believe, they also acquired the power to heal the sick and went on to save people on their own. I believe that many of you will receive the power to save innumerable people. This is the power of faith and the power of the Truths.

When Paul the Apostle suddenly lost his eyesight and began hearing the voice of Jesus Christ, he changed from a persecutor of Christians to a fervent Christian missionary. Just like Saint Paul, many people who are now dubious of Happy Science and hesitant to join will later come to believe in Happy Science after they experience a miracle.

These miracles, these phenomena, will increase by ten- and even a hundredfold from this day. I travel the world to create miracles.

77

I strongly believe that by the time I return to Japan, I will be hearing about numerous miracles happening to the people in the countries I visited. My strong wish to guide people is what causes them to change their lives. They are able to switch their life course from a negative one to a positive one. Doing this, in fact, is the holy purpose and duty of religions.

Why do such miracles occur? In short, it is because of our wish to save humankind, our wish to bring happiness to as many people as possible. The desire to help and save a boundless number of people is what underlies and resides at the root of my teachings. This desire prompts miracles to happen.

OUR MOVEMENT TO BRING GOD'S SALVATION

I visited Brazil in November 2010. To research a little about the country, I watched a few Brazilian movies before going there. However, many of the movies were horrible. They contained an excessive amount of crime, a lot of violence, and many characters who were criminals. The movies depicted a world so appalling that it would have been nearly impossible to imagine that God could exist.

After actually visiting, I saw that São Paulo was more beautiful than its portrayal in the movies. São Paulo was a very urban area and reminded me somewhat of New York City. However, the movies' depiction of the city gave me the impression that São Paulo overflows with crime and that aggression fills its people's hearts. These movies made me think that Brazilians must see crime and aggression as a normal way of life. So as I watched, I felt that I could not possibly leave Brazil as it is.

If a society is ailing and the citizens cannot distinguish right from wrong, and the people do not know of God's salvation, then you must teach them. This is a very noble job. That is why I must give as many teachings as possible about mystical Truths. Our activities must have the power to change the lives of people. So, although it is desirable that more and more people join Happy Science, it is not our only goal.

It is the job of Happy Science to lead people in the correct direction. It is our job to increase the number of people who will live their lives in accordance with God's Will. We have seen a sharp increase in the number of believers. But growth alone is not our only purpose. I implore the members, "You must put your soul into it. You must put your heart into it. Please act with passion. I want you to imbue your actions with a strong wish to save people."

We wish for righteousness to prevail on Earth. It is our deep hope that all people will be connected by love. Happy Science aims to create a society where people do not hate, where people repent for the mistakes they've made and forgive and love one another. To this end, I believe some countries are chosen; they are chosen as countries with strong spiritual energy.

For example, it has only been twenty-four years since we started our activities, and yet Brazil has raced ahead and grown much. While I have not directly guided Brazil, the people have proactively expanded our organization. Members have built the Brazil shoshinkan. I can see how much effort it took to build such a grand temple. I really appreciate how much they have done. The Japanese tend to be doubtful and are slow to act, while the Brazilians are working very hard to spread the Truths. I sometimes tell the Japanese members to look up to the Brazilian members and try to learn from them. They have become a model for members all over the world. This is a very joyous thing that is happening.

Like Brazil, India is making great progress. It is said that by 2013, the number of members will shoot past a million. In India, Happy Science is increasing at a tremendous pace. One in three people who watched *The Rebirth of Buddha*, a movie I produced in 2009, became devotees of Happy Science. They became true believers. I have heard that the movie, which is about Buddha, was well received by the people of India because Buddhism began in India. But I was amazed that just after watching the movie, many people in India became members right on the spot, even though it was an animated film.

SPREADING MIRACLES
FROM THE SPIRIT WORLD

The Laws of Eternity, another movie I produced, became popular in Brazil, where people have a strong interest in spirituality and are eager to know about the spirit world. *The Laws of Eternity* explains the multidimensional structure of the other world and depicts each dimension in detail. That movie is very difficult to understand. I think it's one of the most complicated animated films that I have produced. While the film is beautiful, the content is quite difficult. Many people in Japan are unable to understand the film. Perhaps much of the Japanese population cannot understand the film because many of them do not even believe that the other world or other dimensions exist.

Allan Kardec's *The Spirits' Book* also explains the other world. This book has sold over four million copies in Brazil and reportedly has influenced more than twenty million people. *The Spirits' Book* is a compilation and summary of spiritual messages conveyed to Kardec through automatic writing.

In 1981, I also started to commune with spirits through automatic writing. My hand moved involuntarily and started writing messages from the heavenly realm. This was the beginning of Happy Science. Then, various Divine Spirits of Heaven started to use my vocal cords to speak through me.

Now, about five hundred Guiding Spirits belong to the Happy Science spirit group. In 2010 alone, I published forty-two books to communicate messages I had received from ninety-three spirits. You can see that great spiritual powers support Happy Science. This feat is far greater than what Kardec accomplished with *The Spirit's Book*.

We are publishing books at a rate of one per week. This is a miracle beyond comparison. Moreover, advertisements for these books appear every week in major newspapers in Japan. Indeed, Japan is in the process of changing. However, it breaks my heart to say that the Japanese have not yet reached a point where they would find *The Laws of Eternity* interesting or the different dimensions of the spirit world amazing.

Although it will take some time, I would like to accomplish a complete spiritual revolution in Japan, the motherland of Happy Science. I hope that the philosophy of Happy Science will spread far and wide throughout the world and that the teachings will be reverse-imported back to Japan.

I would like to show the Japanese how enthusiastically people in other countries are studying my teachings and urge them to follow your lead. It is my earnest hope that you will invite many people to join our movement and spread the Truths all over the world. I hope that my passion in this cause has reached you.

Chapter Six

Q&A WITH
MASTER OKAWA

QUESTION 1

ABOUT PREDESTINATION

I would like to ask about destiny. Some people believe that they are destined to live an unhappy life and that their fate cannot change in any way. Could you tell me your thoughts on predestination? Could you also explain how possession by evil spirits can influence people's lives?

ANSWER

First, let me answer your question about destiny. Christianity teaches very little about the spirit world, where the soul dwells prior to life on Earth. So most people have little information about the spirit world or do not believe in it. Nonetheless, we create a rough life plan before we are born. In that sense, every human has a "destiny" to a certain degree.

A rough life plan would include choosing your parents. You choose your birthplace and decide who will make up your close relationships. You also pick, to some degree, what kind of occupation you wish to pursue. In most cases, people have one skill or distinguished ability. So, in that sense, all people, to a certain extent, have a destiny to lead a particular kind of life. However, this is not 100 percent set in stone.

If you could not change your destiny or lead a different life, then being born on Earth would have no meaning; it would make no difference whether you put forth any effort or not. This kind of world would be very cruel. If your efforts on Earth did not amount to anything, then humans would only be lazy and neglectful. Everyone would stop doing anything if putting forth effort and doing nothing amounted to the same result. Doing good deeds would have no point.

Your life definitely has a framework, or a basic direction. However, you are the one who decides what to do and how to develop your life. As a rule of thumb, you have the power to determine about half of your life. The remaining half is divided into two quarters. One of those quarters is determined by the framework—your personality, nature, and plans—that you created for your life before your birth. The other quarter is decided by your encounters with spiritual beings and your experience of spiritual influences while you are on Earth.

Evil spirits may possess you and influence your life. However, you also may come into contact with good spirits such as angels or beings that are close to angels. You can be guided by either evil spirits or Divine Spirits. I said that half of your life is within your control. But through religious training, you will be able to receive guidance from Divine Spirits, and you can increase that number to 75 percent. You could control 75 percent of your life and change the course of your life in the direction you desire.

QUESTION 2

HAVING TWO MISSIONS IN LIFE

I am twenty-eight years old. After reading your books, I have come to understand that in the end, each person has only one path to pursue. I have learned that we have a single mission in life that we truly desire to fulfill. However, I cannot help but feel that I have two missions in life. Is it possible to have two missions in life?

ANSWER

If you are still in your late twenties, it is not unusual for you to have more than two missions. This is because you are young. We are in an era when young people pursue many dreams. When you are in your twenties, it's fine to pursue many things, not just two. Believe in your possibilities and act on them. You have the right to test your potential.

As you get older, your true mission or abilities and talents become clearer and clearer. By the time you are in your forties, you will have to narrow down your choices to just one. Between the ages of forty and fifty, you will want to choose one path. You must narrow it down to one mission. Then, as the years go by, your choices narrow and you are left with one path. So, you just have to think about finding your ultimate path by the time you are in your forties.

Of course, many exceptions exist in today's age. Our life expectancy is rising, and many people start their second or third lives when they are seventy or eighty. Basically, you have no limit on how many missions or dreams you can pursue. It is fine to try out many things. Many people live this way.

However, you must know that although people seem to have many abilities or skills, in the end, they will not reach the top ranks unless they concentrate on improving just one skill. When you attempt to polish two, three or four skills, you will only obtain second-, third-, or fourth-rate results. So if you wish to join the top ranks of a certain field, you must limit yourself to one skill. You should keep that in mind.

For example, I have authored many books so I am quite skilled in writing. If I ever attempt to become a novelist, I think I would, to a certain degree, have the talent to write a good novel. However, it would be difficult for me to join the top ranks of novelists. Why? Because I am a man of religion and I usually think about the ideal way for humans to live. Much of today's literature is the opposite, and contains hellish thoughts and ideas. I don't think I would be able to write on such topics. Since many people find these types of books enticing, I wouldn't be able to author a trendy book. In that sense, although I am a good writer, I don't think I could become a top-ranked novelist. I can help more people by concentrating on preaching the Truths.

In general, it is best to find one skill and pursue it. When you are young, you still have the leeway to try things and make mistakes; you have the right to challenge yourself and come to know yourself. By doing so, you may discover your hidden talents.

If, in your late twenties, you can already narrow yourself to two missions, you are probably more enlightened than others your age. When I was in my twenties, I pursued many, many goals. So, I think it is fine that you have two goals. It means that you are very pure.

Once you are a little older, let's say when you are about fifty years old, you should decide on one path. This will help you find success. However, since today's life expectancy is about eighty years, you may possibly venture onto a second or third new path. I myself started to give lectures over-seas at the age of fifty-one. I thought it would be impossible, but I have spent three years giving lectures in English. Now, just as I can give hour-and-a-half lectures in Japanese, I can do the same in English.

So, you do not have to set the course of your life at this moment, but you should limit it to one path by the time you are fifty years old. Until then, you will probably try out many things and give up on some along the way.

QUESTION 3

OVERCOMING DEPRESSION

Cases of depression are increasing in countries around the world. Is there a spiritual cause for depression? How can we overcome it?

ANSWER

Depression has many causes. In urban areas, because competition is fierce, many people fall into a state of depression when they experience failure or have difficulty achieving their dreams. In some cases, a positive event can bring about depression. For instance, some people experience depression when they receive a promotion, because they feel they do not yet possess the skills required to fill the post. So even though they get promoted, they sink into depression and stop coming to work.

Some people try to ward off their stress by drinking alcohol. I hear that in areas such as the United States or South America, many turn to drugs. People use these substances to numb their rational minds and somehow protect their egos.

If you are experiencing prolonged periods of depression, let us say, longer than three months, then it is likely that evil spirits are influencing you. Your mind has a compass needle, which is capable of pointing in any direction. It can point up toward Heaven or down toward Hell. Just like the hand of a watch, it can spin and stop in any direction. When you are depressed, your compass needle is constantly pointing at one spot in Hell. When your mind persists in the direction of Hell, evil spirits from Hell will resonate with your mind's vibrations and try to possess you.

Depression can sometimes lead to suicide. The souls of people who commit suicide cannot return immediately to Heaven. Before moving on, these souls usually roam around Earth for about the same number of years they had left in life. During that time, these lost souls search out and possess people who are similar to them. Then, they try to repeat their suicide through the person they have possessed, and drag him or her into Hell.

It is the job of religions to help prevent suicides. Of course, doctors try to cure depression through medicine. They also may isolate the depressed patient from other people. But none of these medical treatments provide a fundamental cure. In order to cure depression at its root, you must learn to generate your own energy. Don't rely on a power plant to send you electricity; you must create energy inside your own house with your own power generator. You must use the power generator within your mind to create energy on your own. It is vital to develop the strength to do this.

How do you generate this energy on your own? How can you maintain a positive state of mind? How do you create energy so you can shine brightly?

First, you must try to cultivate deeper gratitude. Depressed people tend to have very little gratitude toward those around them. They need to be thankful for the help they have received from other people. People with depression have to realize that countless people have taken care of them. A heart full of gratitude will help them understand that they have been extremely blessed by many things.

Depression is prevalent all over the world. So, it is very important that we all have gratitude for everything we have been given. For example, some people may think that they are unfortunate to have been born human. But humans are far happier than animals. Humans are given much greater freedom. We should all be grateful for this. Most animals cannot speak. They cannot open bank accounts. Animals are never paid a salary. Police dogs work hard but they receive no pay. Because we are human, we are able to receive some kind of a salary for our work. We are given economic freedom because we are human. Being human is a very noble thing that we should all be thankful for. So it is vital to change your perspective and look at how much you have been given. Also, you must not give in to drugs or alcohol so easily. A heart of gratitude is the first step toward curing depression.

I also would recommend self-reflection to people who are depressed. However, if they go straight into self-reflection, there's a danger that they might condemn themselves even further and sink deeper into their depressed state. So, before repenting, it is very important that you strengthen your belief that you are a child of God. This is the second point. Always tell yourself that you are a child of light and created by God. A strong awareness that you are God's child will help you realize how important you truly are.

I think that Christian teachings are wonderful. But the concept of "original sin" is so deeply engraved into Christianity, that many people really believe that they are children of sin. They just can't come around to see the bright, positive side of life. However, just by simply changing your perspective, the world becomes filled with wondrous things.

Take, for example, a highway, littered with trash. If you only look at the trash, you would think the highway was filthy. However, if you keep driving, eventually you will reach a piece of highway that is free of trash. So by turning your eyes away from the trash and looking toward the clean road, the world will look entirely different to you. Think about what it is you are currently looking at. If you are always seeing the dark, negative side of the world, change the direction that your mind is facing and try to look at the bright, happy side of the world. It is important to make this effort.

Countless people think they have absolutely no good qualities. Depressed people, especially, tend to feel this way. However, if you ponder it deeply, you realize that this isn't true. If you can't find your good qualities, ask people around you to point them out. They will instantly list five or six great characteristics. It should be easy to point out the good points of others. However, those who always look at their bad points cannot see their own good points. You must accept your good points with an open heart. This will prompt you to generate your own energy.

Once your life starts picking up and moving in a positive direction, the next step is to accumulate small experiences of success. Don't aim to accomplish something grand. It is important to succeed in many small tasks to gain self-confidence. Then, you will be able to store up enough strength to humbly reflect on your mistakes. I think it is important to take these steps.

Another point is to avoid comparing yourself to other people. An endless number of people will always be better than you. Of course, many people will be inferior to you as well. It is important to find someone who is superior to you in your area of interest, and aim to become like him or her. However, just because the other person is superior to you doesn't mean that you are worthless. If you have a tendency to think this way, you must change it.

If someone is more successful than you are in your area of interest, you must bless that person. You should bless his or her success and wish to become like him or her. If you can praise that person, then you are taking a step closer to becoming like him or her. Try to think this way and bless people. Have the heart to bless those who are successful. This is an effective remedy for depression. It is important to take courage to praise others who have succeeded.

ABOUT BEING VEGETARIAN

Is it right to be vegetarian?
Is it wrong to eat meat?

Ever since Plato, some western religions have presented the view that the spirit and the body are separate. They also believe that only humans have souls, and that animals don't. This belief has been predominant for quite a long time in the West. People who eat meat tend to believe that animals don't have souls. However, people in Eastern cultures such as India believe that animals also have souls. Ancient Indian belief even states that the soul alternately reincarnates between human bodies and animal bodies.

In truth, human souls basically reincarnate only as humans. Nonetheless, animals also

103

have souls, although they are less developed than human souls. They have souls that experience different emotions, and feel delight, anger, sorrow, and pleasure. So I don't think it is necessarily right to say that we can eat animals simply because they don't have souls.

Some may say, then, that we should all become vegetarians. However, plants also have souls. Plants cannot move actively like animals, but if you videotape plants with a time-lapse camera, you'll see that they are indeed moving, if only very slowly. They are alive. They rejoice when the rain falls after a hot day or when the sun shines after a continuous spell of cloudy weather. So even plants feel simple emotions such as delight and sorrow.

Saying this, however, will only make it difficult for humans to live. You would not be able to eat either animals or plants. It would no longer be an issue of whether you should become a vegetarian or not—you wouldn't be able to eat anything at all. If you couldn't eat anything at all and died, then God creating humans in this world would have no meaning. You'd have to survive by eating stones and rocks. In fact, minerals are also alive. They grow much slower than plants. Nevertheless they form crystals over millions and billions of years. They actually live for a very long period of time. Essentially, everything in this world is endowed with life.

Cultural differences exist over what you eat and don't eat. But it does not make sense to use the existence of a soul, or the lack of it, as the criterion to judge whether you should eat something or not. Humans are the most highly developed souls among the life forms on Earth. We eat other animals and plants, and this may appear to be a cruel thing to do. However, viewed from a different perspective, animals and plants are helping humans experience life and achieve spiritual growth. By offering themselves as nourishment, they are undergoing very noble soul training.

Whether you are a vegetarian or not, it is important that you give gratitude when you eat. You may feel the guilt of taking a life. But you can make up for it by having a heart full of gratitude, and by living and working in a way that will make the loss of these creatures' precious lives worthwhile. If the way you live can add worth to their taken lives by five to ten times, I am sure they will be happy.

I do not say whether it is right or wrong to be a vegetarian based on the existence or nonexistence of souls. It requires many sacrifices to sustain human life. I believe that we can add value to these precious sacrifices through the efforts we make to create a better society.

THE DUTIES OF POLITICIANS

*How can I, as a politician, bring
happiness to the citizens of this country?
How can I contribute to their happiness?*

ANSWER

Being a politician requires a lot of creativity. You cannot do your job simply by imitating what others have done before you. Because of the creative nature of their jobs, politicians enjoy great opportunities to actualize their visions of the future. If you are a state representative, you have the extremely important role of designing and shaping the future of the country and turning visions and dreams into reality. This is a difficult job. People will judge you on your achievements. No one knows beforehand whether your ideas are right or whether they will produce good results. People will judge your work only after looking at the results of your efforts.

So first, it is important that you paint a vision of the future. Second, you should look at the resources that are available to you, such as budgets, citizens, industries, and natural resources, and think about what you can create using these resources. An important part of a politician's job is to use the resources that are available in this world to create pieces of art with unlimited potential. So, take a look at what is within your reach right now, and think about the beautiful pieces of artwork that could be formed out of it.

Please remember that you have an important job and that the politicians' duties are very close to the works of God. Materialism and atheism have affected a great number of people. In the end, however, politicians have only God to rely on, and many of them work every day with prayers in their hearts. The higher their positions, the more intensively they pray to God because they are in a position to work on behalf of God.

That is why I hope that you will find time to practice meditation in silence. Through spiritual discipline, you can train yourself to hear the voices of God, Heaven, and the Divine Spirits, and receive their guidance and the visions they send you. Religious activities will not work against your occupation. Religious discipline will help you fulfill your duties as a politician. Top leaders must strive to be closer to God. Put another way, politicians must have virtue. What does it mean to be a person of virtue? It means that you are capable of loving many people, that your heart has the capacity to accept many people.

In Japan, many politicians belong to religions. However, most of them join only to win the votes of the members. Still, a conscientious few believe that they are not qualified to govern the country unless they have a mind that is close to the mind of God. I hope that you will become a politician who will serve as a great strength for your country, and open a door to a brighter future.

ABOUT CAPITAL PUNISHMENT

*More than half of convicted murderers
become repeat offenders. Since human
life is eternal, we could conclude that
the offender should leave this world and
try again in a next life. Then, people's
lives would not be disrupted, leading to
the happiness of the majority. But this
way of thinking can be dangerous.
What are your thoughts on the
death penalty?*

ANSWER

Many religions preach against capital punishment. I suppose it's natural that they are against
the death penalty. However if we look comprehensively at the subject and take the spiritual
perspective into consideration as well, I think it is

a matter of degree. It would be too much to apply the death penalty to someone if there is room for sympathy. For example, if someone committed a crime under circumstances that couldn't be helped, the death penalty should be avoided.

In Muslim countries, the death sentence can be quickly imposed on someone who violates Islamic law. If the person committed a minor offense, I believe that the death penalty would be an extreme punishment. We should look at the balance between the punishment and the crime.

In Central and South America, I hear that the crime rate is immensely high. In Peru, the recidivism rate of those who are released from prisons also is very high. For that reason, the Happy Science minister in Peru frequently visits prisons to preach our teachings. The goal is to teach the Truths while the prisoners are still jailed so that they will not commit crimes when they are released.

Many people commit crimes out of ignorance. These people probably blame the environment they grew up in, and think they are suffering because of the world and people around them. You can awaken these people by teaching them the Truths.

But in the case of atrocious crimes, such as school shootings in which dozens of elementary school students are killed on their way home, parents may not easily forgive the shooter. We also have to take the perspective of deterrence into consideration. If all murders, under any circumstances, were immune from capital punishment, it would be difficult to discourage crime.

Of course, situations exist in which the taking of a life happens out of self-defense. If an armed robber comes into your house and tries to kill you, you must defend yourself. But if malicious and brutal crimes grow prevalent—if murderous acts such as armed bank robberies that kill many, random people become too common—then I feel that we need to conduct careful deliberation. Under these conditions, abolishing the death penalty probably would not help bring down the crime rate.

If possible, I would like to teach criminals the Truths and tell them, "What you're doing is an act of evil and you will suffer many hundreds of years in Hell for it." But until the Truths become prevalent throughout society, the least we can do is prevent Hell from expanding any further. It would be undesirable to deprive good, decent people of their lives.

When I went to Brazil, I noticed that iron fences surrounded many buildings in São Paulo. It's a sight you don't see in Tokyo. These iron fences around the buildings probably exist because people try to break in. Banks, too, have iron fences around them to keep the burglars and robbers out. Compared to world standards, Brazil's crime rate is high and the country is, apparently, unsafe.

An effective police force could prevent crime. Still, unless we can lessen the number of people who only think about themselves, we will not be able to reduce the number of criminal acts.

I think we should take different measures depending on the condition of the country. For example, in Japan, there was an era called the Heian period about a thousand years ago. During this time, peace lasted several hundred years and reportedly not a single death sentence was carried out. This period in history demonstrates that peace is possible in society.

The answer to your question differs depending on the state of a country's conditions, such as its culture, its quality of life, and its morals. But in high-crime countries, I think the death penalty should not be abolished so quickly. It should be kept to protect the good citizens of that country. We need to take the circumstances into consideration when delivering the sentence. If no one was ever sentenced to death no matter how many people they murdered, some people would actually decide to kill others. So, in order to protect the good citizens, I feel that we should not abolish the death penalty completely.

From a spiritual perspective, those who commit the crime of murder will most likely go to Hell after death. However, their sin is actually lessened when they are executed for their crime. It is like paying back part of the debt. History's war heroes, who killed many people, often died at the hands of others. The spirits of these war heroes have told me that getting killed, in the end, made their sins lighter. This is the Law of Karma, or the Law of Cause, Condition, Result, and Reward. You can lessen the negative aspect of your karma by experiencing the same event you inflicted on others

Those who fight in the name of justice, such as police officers or soldiers in war, are exempt from this principle. For instance, an on-duty policeman who becomes involved in a gunfight and kills a criminal will not fall to Hell for his action. From the perspective of the Truths, it is the leader—the politician, the king, or the president—who will bear responsibility for this act, not the individuals acting in accordance with the law.

Overall, I feel that, for the sake of crime prevention, the death penalty should not be abolished in countries where atrocious crimes occur. I hope that in the near future, we will be able to deter crime by spreading the Truths throughout society. I would like to lower the crime rate by providing the teachings in prisons as well.

While it is true that criminals can lessen the weight of their sins in the afterlife by paying the price of their crimes in this world, this is far from ideal. Such a situation is far from the utopian society we are aiming to create. I pray that the number of iron fences will decrease around the world.

I would like for this planet to become a peaceful and safe world. It's better for all of us. So let's work to create a more peaceful world. The golden rule in the world of religion is "Do unto others as you would have others do unto you." To put it another way, "Do not do to others what you would not want others to do to you." If you don't want to be killed, you shouldn't kill other people. If you don't want others to steal your belongings, then you should not steal. This is the golden rule. This is the fundamental sense of morality. This should be the common sense that we put in practice in daily life.

Still, I think that the government is responsible for securing public safety, and it is their duty to protect its good citizens. We should allow law enforcement agencies to have the power to enforce the law. Even in Japan, where crime is low, occasionally incidents occur in which psychopaths murder many innocent people. We probably should not abolish the death penalty yet. We need to keep it to deter crime.

Of course, it will be best if we can persuade people through words. However, even in Brazil, where 80 percent of the population is Catholic, the crime rate is very high. They haven't been able to resolve this paradox. While many people in Brazil and elsewhere have faith in God, religion does not have real power in solving this issue. This is probably because many have heard of Heaven and Hell, but very few have actually felt the presence of the other world or have had spiritual experiences.

Our ultimate goal is to create a peaceful and heavenly society on this planet. To this end, we must make actual efforts to reduce crime. We must resolve the issue of poverty, which is the breeding ground of crime. In order to lessen poverty, we must attempt to improve politics and the economy. At the same time, we must continue our religious efforts to spread the Truths through our spiritual movement. We will not be able to solve this issue unless we tackle it from both the worldly and spiritual approaches. In conclusion, as of now, I think that we are not ready to abolish capital punishment completely.

Question 7

Definition of the Antichrist

The Book of Revelation talks about the Antichrist. It also says that many people will follow the Antichrist. What sort of person is the Antichrist?

Answer

People have different ideas about the Antichrist. Looking back on the two-thousand-year history of the Christian Church, I think the concept of the Antichrist served as a convenient way to describe someone who raised an opinion that did not fit the Church's. But I feel that we must alter the way we help and save people as times change. Maintaining the original teachings is beneficial in some respects, but I do not believe that all new religions established after Christianity are against Jesus Christ's teachings.

It seems that over the course of the years, the Church has edited Jesus's thoughts in the Bible. This is especially true with regard to Jesus's teachings about the spiritual, which he talked about a lot when he was alive. Some of the spiritual occurrences he mentioned are retained in the Bible today. For example, the Bible often references chasing out evil spirits. It is also written in the Bible that Jesus said, "Elijah has already come," (Matt. 9:11), which reveals that John the Baptist was the reincarnation of Elijah. So if you read Jesus's words that have been preserved in the Bible, you will notice that he acknowledged spiritual powers and the concept of reincarnation between this world and the other world.

Many spiritual philosophies emerged afterward, but every one of them faced persecution for heresy. True, some of them *were* heretical, but others shared common ideas with other world religions. It was a mixture of wheat and chaff. They included both right and wrong beliefs.

I believe the criterion with which to judge whether a religion is good or bad lies in the words Jesus spoke: "A tree is identified by its fruit. If a tree is good, its fruit will be good. If a tree is bad, its fruit will be bad" (Matt. 12:33).

If the people who believe in a particular faith are unrespectable, then they may be considered what the Bible calls the Antichrist. If, on the other hand, people who believe in the teachings enter the right path, the path of right faith and the path to glory, then the fruit must be good. Without the support of many people, they cannot receive recognition in society. This is true not only with religions, but also with corporations and other businesses. So in the end, I think that the ultimate criterion to judge whether a spiritual movement represents the Antichrist is to look at the fruit, the results, of the actions of its people.

ABOUT EL CANTARE

What kind of being is Lord El Cantare?

ANSWER

"El Cantare" means "the light of Earth." El Cantare is a Grand Spirit that has the goal of bringing happiness to all living creatures on Earth, and making the whole Earth shine with light. Today, the core consciousness of El Cantare's immense life energy has taken human form again and was born as Ryuho Okawa.

I, the person you see before you, with the name Ryuho Okawa, am not El Cantare in His entirety. The mission of El Cantare's spiritual existence is too grand to inhabit a physical body. A human body cannot carry out all El Cantare's functions and roles. A large portion of El Cantare's soul exists in Heaven. What I can do as a human is limited. I have far greater power as a spiritual being.

So the complete being called El Cantare is composed of the part of His soul that dwells in my physical body on Earth and the larger portion of His soul that exists in Heaven. You can understand El Cantare as a being that is related to and has guided all major religions in this world.

For more on El Cantare, I would like you to refer to the other books I have published.

THE GRAND SPIRIT, EL CANTARE

"El" means "light" and "Cantare" means "the great land" or "the planet Earth," which makes the whole name mean "Earth that is brimming with light." El Cantare bears ultimate responsibility and makes the final decisions on the fate of humankind.

Earth's spirit group consists of a congregation of spirits known as Divine Spirits. Among them are spirits who have progressed to such a high state of excellence that they are known as gods. These spirits are divinities who retain human character. El Cantare is the highest Grand Spirit of Earth's spirit group and holds the highest authority among them. He has been responsible for guiding Earth since before the creation of humankind.

El Cantare is a being that combines God and Buddha. The word "Buddha" originally meant "Awakened One" or "Enlightened One." It is often used to refer to Gautama Siddhartha, also known as Shakyamuni Buddha, who achieved enlightenment while on Earth. The historical Shakyamuni Buddha was in fact a past life of El Cantare. A part of El Cantare's immense life energy had incarnated onto Earth as Shakyamuni Buddha. The word "Buddha" is also used to refer to the Creator of the Grand Cosmos, the Primordial God.

Of course, other Grand Spirits that guide Earth also exist in the ninth dimension in Heaven. They have agreed to cooperate with and support Happy Science, which was established by El Cantare, who continues to lead the movement. In this context, Happy Science is an organization that was not created by human beings. It was established through the consensus of the Grand Spirits of Heaven. Happy Science's mission is to bring salvation to all humankind by spreading the universal Truths of God that El Cantare preaches.

If you wonder how best to describe the being that is El Cantare, it is probably easiest to think of Him as a combination of Buddha and Christ. As El Cantare, Master Okawa preaches God's Truths while simultaneously expounding teachings of love and salvation. His mission is to spread Buddha's teachings of enlightenment while also preaching Christ's messages of love. El Cantare has emerged on Earth to bridge the East and West together, to bring salvation to all humankind.

QUESTION 9

BELIEVING IN THE LORD

We, the members of Happy Science, truly believe in the descent of the lord. But why is it that the leaders of other religious organizations do not believe in it?

ANSWER

I believe it is simply a matter of the number of years that passed. It has only been twenty-four years since I established Happy Science, so it will take some time for them to believe what we say. For example, Jesus Christ officially started preaching when he was about thirty years old and continued for only three years until he died at the age of thirty-three. When Jesus died, he had almost no disciples. Today, two thousand years later, billions of Christians across the globe believe in him. With hindsight, it is hard to imagine that people didn't believe in Jesus when he was alive. However, people didn't think then that Christianity would develop into one of the world's largest religions.

You may ask why people do not believe in El Cantare, but at no time in history have people believed in a savior right away. It even took Buddhism hundreds of years to spread around the world. Today, the transportation system and mass media have developed greatly, and information is quickly spread throughout the world. Despite this, it will take a certain amount of time for this Truth to reach every corner of the Earth. Those who have faith in preexisting religions may find it hard to abandon their faith and convert to a new religion. It's inevitable that it will take time.

Those who find faith in new religions can acknowledge established religions, but those who believe in established religions find it difficult to accept new religions. Something similar to this happened in the relationship between Christianity and Islam. I won't expand on it too much since it is complicated, but Christianity and Islam are said to be brother religions. Indeed, these religions are similar in many respects.

Muhammad actually acknowledged Jesus Christ as well as the Bible. He created the Koran fully accepting both the Old Testament and the New Testament. So Islam accepts Christianity, but Christianity, being the predecessor, cannot accept Islam. Dante, an Italian poet, wrote a story about the spirit world in *The Divine Comedy*. According to him, both Muhammad and Shakyamuni Buddha have fallen to Hell. He said that all religious founders, other than Jesus Christ, have fallen to Hell. However, the fact is that numerous Divine Spirits were born on Earth to lead different countries, so I think that his thinking was rather closed-minded.

It is always difficult for preexisting religions to accept a religion that comes into existence after them. For example, the Jews found it difficult to believe in Christianity because Judaism existed prior to Christianity. Even today, Jews see Jesus Christ as a prophet, not as a messiah. In the Islamic faith, Muhammad called himself the last prophet. From the Muslim point of view, there have been no more prophets since the sixth or seventh century, and no more prophets will ever appear. To Muslims, all religions that were created after Islam are wrong.

When people convert to a new faith, conflicts occur between those with the new faith and those with the preexisting faith. Just as Jesus said, "Do not think that I have come to bring peace to the Earth; I have not come to bring peace, but a sword" (Matt. 10:34–39). This means that if, for example, someone of Jewish faith in your family converted to Christianity, it would cause strife within your family. Jesus described these conflicts as "bringing a sword."

Humans have a tendency to believe in things that existed before them. In order to prove what we believe is right, we have no other choice but to take time spreading the teachings. Those of you who believe in this new faith must awaken to your duty and responsibility to spread the Truths. I hope that you will continue to make an effort so that many people will accept and support our movement.

AFTERWORD

I have never before felt the gravity of the phrase "once in a lifetime" as heavily as I did during my tour in Brazil. The tour took place during a year of many personal challenges. I gave a total of 229 talks in 2010, and published fifty-two store-released books between November 2009 and October 2010. This publication record is now listed in *Guinness World Records* as the most books written in one year by an individual.

You might feel the zeal of that year rise from these pages like the smoke of kindling flames. The weight of my own words and my sense of mission as a world savior and world teacher have made me ever stronger as a person and have inspired a great many people. This book is my declaration to the world that

I will spread these teachings throughout every corner of the globe.

Ryuho Okawa

Founder and CEO

Happy Science Group

January 2011

The contents of this book were compiled from the following lectures:

Chapter 1: Your Path to Happiness
"The Way to Happiness" [Kōfuku e no Michi]
November 10, 2010 in Jundiai, Brazil

Chapter 2: Awaken Your Soul to God's Truths
"Awakening to the Truth" [Shinjitsu e no Mezame]
November 12, 2010 in São Paulo, Brazil

Chapter 3: Angels Dispel Darkness and Spread Love
"On Love and the Work of Angels" [Ai to Tenshi no Hataraki]
November 14, 2010 in São Paulo, Brazil

Chapter 4: Invincible Thinking Can Turn Struggles into Success
"The Power of Invincible Thinking" [Jōshō Shikō no Chikara]
November 9, 2010 in Sorocaba, Brazil

Chapter 5: Opening the Door to Miracles
"On Mystical Power" [Shinpi no Chikara ni Tsuite]
November 7, 2010 in São Paulo, Brazil

Chapter 6: Q&A with Master Okawa
Q1 About Predestination; November 10, 2010 in Jundiai, Brazil
Q2 Having Two Missions in Life; November 12, 2010 in São Paulo, Brazil
Q3 Overcoming Depression; November 10, 2010 in Jundiai, Brazil
Q4 About Being Vegetarian; November 9, 2010 in Sorocaba, Brazil
Q5 The Duties of Politicians; November 10, 2010 in Jundiai, Brazil
Q6 About Capital Punishment; November 12, 2010 in São Paulo, Brazil
Q7 Definition of the Antichrist; November 9, 2010 in Sorocaba, Brazil
Q8 About El Cantare; November 10, 2010 in Jundiai, Brazil
Section "The Grand Spirit, El Cantare"
From *The Truth of the Spirit World* [Reiteki Sekai no Hontō no Hanashi] and *The Mystical Laws* [Shinpi no Hō]
Q9 Believing in the Lord; November 9, 2010 in Sorocaba, Brazil

ABOUT THE AUTHOR

Master Ryuho Okawa started receiving messages from great historical figures—Jesus, Buddha, and others from Heaven—in 1981. These holy beings came to him with impassioned messages of urgency, entreating him to deliver their holy wisdom to people on Earth. His calling to become a spiritual leader, to inspire people all over the world with the long-hidden spiritual Truths of the origin of humankind and the soul, was revealed. These conversations unveiled the mysteries of Heaven and Hell and became the foundation on which Master Okawa built his spiritual philosophy. As his spiritual awareness deepened, he came to understand that this wisdom contained the power to help humankind overcome religious and cultural conflicts and usher in an era of peace and harmony on Earth. Just before his thirtieth birthday, Master Okawa left his promising career in business and dedicated himself to publishing the messages he receives from Heaven. Since then, he has published more than seven hundred books (as of April 2011) and become a best-selling author in Japan.

The universality of the wisdom he shares, the depth of his religious and spiritual philosophy, and the clarity and compassion of his messages continue to attract hundreds of millions of readers. In addition to his ongoing writing, Master Okawa gives public talks and lectures throughout the world.

ABOUT HAPPY SCIENCE

In 1986, Master Ryuho Okawa founded Happy Science, a spiritual movement dedicated to bringing greater happiness to humankind by overcoming barriers of race, religion, and culture and by working toward the ideal of a world united in peace and harmony. Supported by followers who live in accordance with Master Okawa's words of enlightened wisdom, Happy Science has grown rapidly since its beginnings in Japan and now extends throughout the world. Today, it has more than twelve million members around the globe, with faith centers in New York, Los Angeles, San Francisco, Tokyo, London, Sydney, São Paulo, and Seoul, among many other major cities. Master Okawa speaks weekly at Happy Science centers and travels around the world giving public lectures. Happy Science provides a variety of programs and services to support local communities and people in need. These programs include preschools, after-school educational programs for youths, and services for senior citizens and the disabled. Members also participate in social and charitable activities, which in the past have included providing relief aid to earthquake victims in Chile and China, raising funds for a charity school in India, and donating mosquito nets to hospitals in Uganda.

PROGRAMS AND EVENTS

Happy Science faith centers offer regular events, programs, and seminars. Join our meditation sessions, video lectures, study groups, seminars, and book events. Our programs will help you:

- Deepen your understanding of the purpose and meaning of life
- Improve your relationships as you learn how to love unconditionally
- Learn how to calm your mind even on stressful days through the practice of contemplation and meditation
- Learn how to overcome life's challenges
  ... and much more.

INTERNATIONAL SEMINARS

Each year, friends from all over the world join our international seminars, held at our faith centers in Japan.

Different programs are offered each year and cover a wide variety of topics, including improving relationships, practicing the Eightfold Path to enlightenment, and loving yourself, to name just a few.

HAPPY SCIENCE MONTHLY

Read Master Okawa's latest lectures in our monthly booklet, *Happy Science Monthly*. You'll also find stories of members' life-changing experiences, news from Happy Science members around the world, in-depth information about Happy Science movies, book reviews, and much more. *Happy Science Monthly* is available in English, Portuguese, Spanish, French, German, Chinese, Korean, and other languages. Back issues are available upon request. Subscribe by contacting the Happy Science location nearest you.

CONTACT INFORMATION

Happy Science is a worldwide organization with faith centers around the globe. For a comprehensive list of centers, visit the worldwide directory at www.happy-science.org or www.happyscience-usa.org.

The following are some of the many Happy Science locations:

UNITED STATES

New York

79 Franklin Street,
New York, NY 10013
Phone: 212-343-7972   Fax: 212-343-7973
Email: ny@happy-science.org
Website: www.happyscience-ny.org

Los Angeles

1590 E. Del Mar Boulevard,
Pasadena, CA 91106
Phone: 626-395-7775   Fax: 626-395-7776
Email: la@happy-science.org
Website: www.happyscience-la.org

San Francisco
525 Clinton Street,
Redwood City, CA 94062
Phone/Fax: 650-363-2777
Email: sf@happy-science.org
Website: www.happyscience-sf.org

New Jersey Temple
Email: nj@happy-science.org
Florida Temple
Email: florida@happy-science.org
Chicago Temple
Email: chicago@happy-science.org
Kauai Temple
Email: kauai-hi@happy-science.org
Hawaii Temple
Email: hi@happy-science.org

INTERNATIONAL
London
3 Margaret Street,
London, W1W 8RE, UK
Phone: 44-20-7323-9255

Fax: 44-20-7323-9344
Email: eu@happy-science.org
Website: www.happyscience-eu.org

Tokyo
1-6-7 Togoshi, Shinagawa,
Tokyo, 142-0041 Japan
Phone: 81-3-6384-5770 Fax: 81-3-6384-5776
Email: tokyo@happy-science.org
Website: www.kofuku-no-kagaku.or.jp/en

Toronto Temple
Email: toronto@happy-science.org
Vancouver Temple
Email: vancouver@happy-science.org
Sydney Temple
Email: sydney@happy-science.org
Bondi Temple (Sydney)
Email: bondi@happy-science.org
Melbourne Temple
Email: melbourne@happy-science.org
New Zealand Temple
Email: newzealand@happy-science.org